MAKERSPACE MODELS

BUILD YOUR OWN ROCKETS AND PLANES

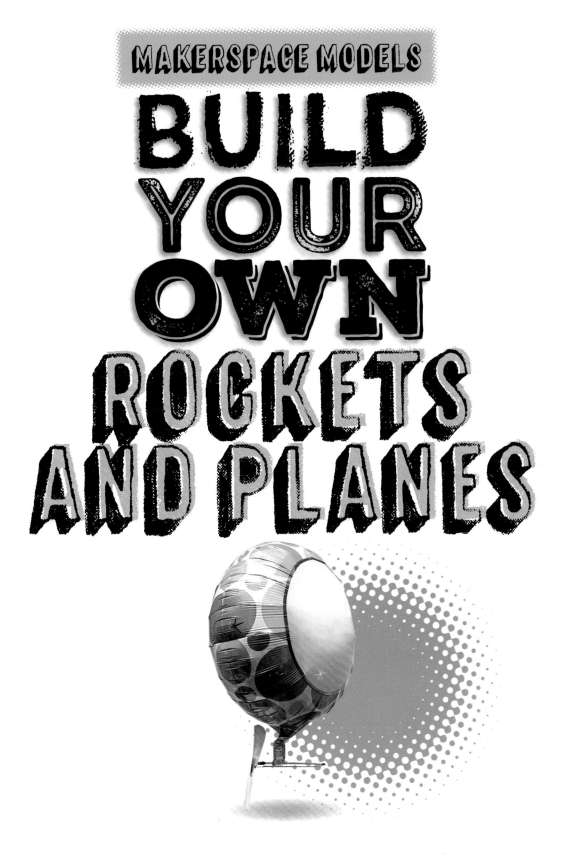

Thanks to the creative team:
Senior Editor: Alice Peebles
Fact checking: Tom Jackson
Design: Perfect Bound Ltd

Hungry Tomato®
A division of Lerner Publishing Group, Inc.
241 First Avenue North
Minneapolis, MN 55401 USA

For reading levels and more information, look up
this title at www.lernerbooks.com.

Main body text set in Neutraliser Serif Regular 9.75/13.

Library of Congress Cataloging-in-Publication Data

The Cataloging-in-Publication Data for *Build Your Own Rockets
and Planes* is on file at the Library of Congress.
ISBN 978-1-5124-5967-8 (lib. bdg.)
ISBN 978-1-5124-9869-1 (EB pdf)

Manufactured in the United States of America
1-43026-27695-9/12/2017

MAKERSPACE MODELS

BUILD YOUR OWN

ROCKETS and PLANES

BY **ROB IVES**

HUNGRY TOMATO®
Minneapolis

SAFETY FIRST

Take care and use good sense when making these fun model aircraft—they are all straightforward, but some activities call for cutting materials, drilling holes, and other skills for which you should ask an adult assistant for help (see below).

Every project includes a list of supplies that you will need. Most will be stuff that you can find around the house or buy inexpensively online or at a local hardware store.

We have also included "How It Works" for each model, to explain in simple terms the engineering or scientific principles that make it work. And for some there is a "Real-World Engineering" snippet that applies these principles to actual machines.

Watch out for this sign accompanying some model instructions. You may need help from an adult with completing these tasks.

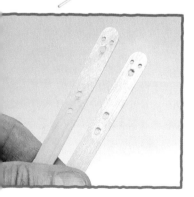

DISCLAIMER

CONTENTS

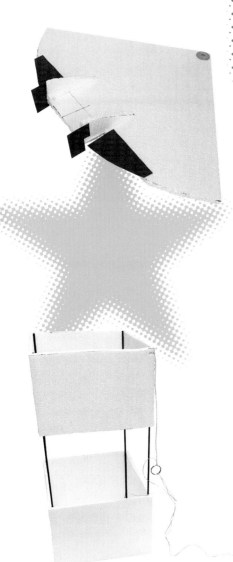

AIRCRAFT

Isn't it amazing how a big, heavy object can get up in the air and stay there? Of course, it took a while for inventors to get that to happen, with lots of experimenting along the way. Some of them started by making birdlike wings and flapping them. Inventors are still perfecting their designs!

Now you can be your own inventor with these eight cool models based on all kinds of aircraft from those early days onward. Even though they're obviously small and very light, they still won't stay up without the right engineering. None of the models has engine power, so find out how they do it!

Take your box kite outdoors and see just how high this high flyer can reach, launch a helicopter, or watch your glider go—and keep on going! The airship might not make a transatlantic flight, as the most powerful ones did, but it may go *much* farther than you expect, and it can certainly hover!

So get your tools and materials together, start building, and see how these craft float and fly like the birds—the best fliers of all . . .

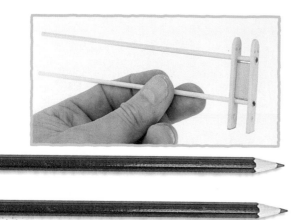

TOP TIPS

- Before you start on any of the models, read the step-by-step instructions all the way through to get an idea of what you're aiming for. The pictures show what the steps tell you to do.

- Some projects need pencils to be cut into sections. Ask an adult for help with this. Use a cutting mat or similar surface to cut on. An efficient way to do it is to cut each face of the pencil in turn with a utility knife, then snap it apart. Clean up any unevenness with the knife.

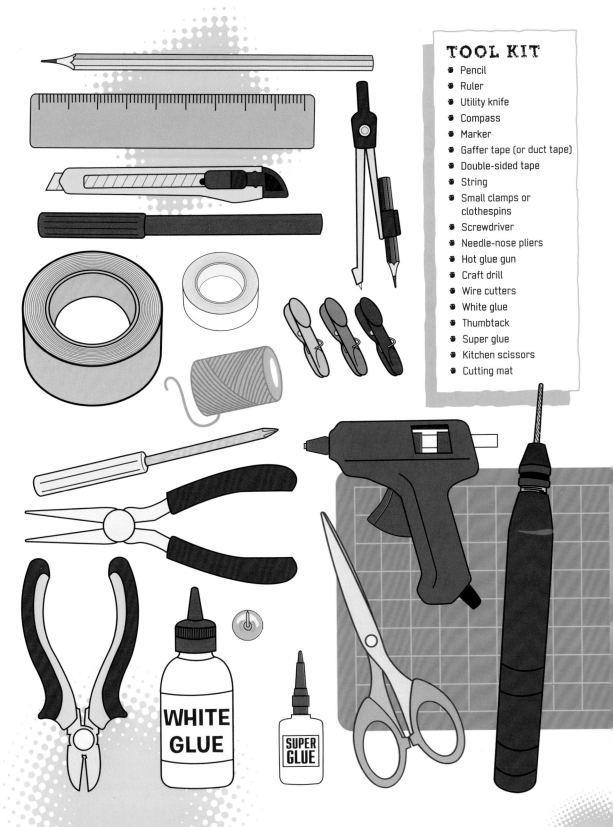

TOOL KIT

- Pencil
- Ruler
- Utility knife
- Compass
- Marker
- Gaffer tape (or duct tape)
- Double-sided tape
- String
- Small clamps or clothespins
- Screwdriver
- Needle-nose pliers
- Hot glue gun
- Craft drill
- Wire cutters
- White glue
- Thumbtack
- Super glue
- Kitchen scissors
- Cutting mat

WHITE GLUE

SUPER GLUE

GLIDING ALONG

YOU WILL NEED:

No engine noise and fabulous flying—that's what's great about gliders. Let those air currents do the work!

TOOLS:

- String
- Scissors
- Marker
- Long ruler
- Utility knife
- Hot glue gun

Large washer or coin

Thin card stock

Polystyrene sheet, 16 x 24 x 0.4 in. (400 x 600 x 10mm)

1 Starting from one corner of the polystyrene sheet, mark out a quarter circle using the string looped around the pen as shown. (The width of the sheet is the radius of the circle.)

2 Mark off about 14 in. (360 mm) centrally along the edge of the quarter cirle, to get an arc. Mark a central tail section, 4.7 in. (120 mm) wide.

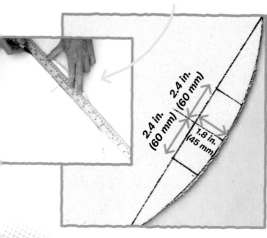

2.4 in. (60 mm)
2.4 in. (60 mm)
2.4 in. (60 mm)
1.8 in. (45 mm)

fin

fin

tail

3 Cut off the two pieces next to the tail to use as tail fins. Use the construction guides on the facing page to cut out two flaps and two rudders from thin card stock. Check that they will fit on as shown in step 5.

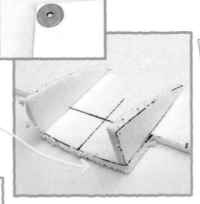

4 Use a hot glue gun to glue the polystyrene fins to the tail.

Glue a large washer or coin to the nose of the glider.

5 Glue the card flaps to the glider body and the rudders to the tail fins as shown.

Hold the glider at head height and let it fall forward from your hand— there's no need to throw it.

WHEEEE!

You'll need plenty of space—it will fly for 100 ft. (30 m)!

HOW IT WORKS

The glider is made from polystyrene, a very **low-density** material. Its large surface area means that there is a lot of **air resistance** pushing upward to keep it airborne. But because it is very thin, it cuts easily through the air. The small weight on the front of the glider helps to keep it moving forward.

REAL-WORLD ENGINEERING

A glider has to fly fast enough for its wings to produce the **lift** needed to keep it in the air. It can gain speed by aiming slightly downward. It also uses **thermals**, columns of warm air rising from the ground, to counteract its descending glide and stay in the air.

BOO-OO-OO-MERANG

The boomerang is an iconic hunting weapon used with great skill by Aboriginal hunters in Australia. It's depicted in some of the world's oldest rock art.

TOOLS:
- Ruler
- String
- Cutting mat
- Thumbtack
- Pencil
- Utility knife

YOU WILL NEED:

A large piece of corrugated cardboard, about 14 in. (350 mm) wide

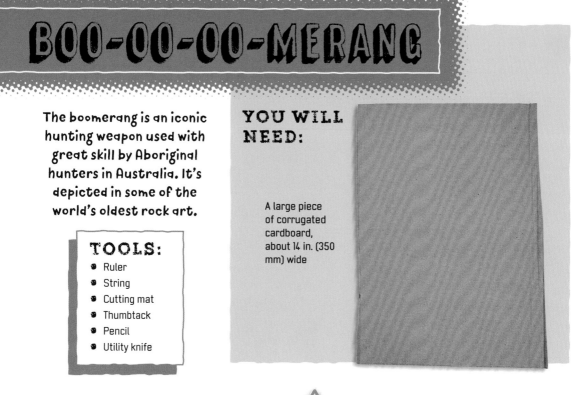

1 Cut a piece of string just less than half the width of your cardboard. Tie a loop in both ends. Lay the cardboard on the cutting mat and press the thumbtack into the center, catching one loop on your string. With the pencil inside the other loop, draw a large circle by keeping the string tight.

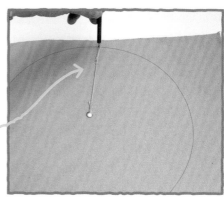

2 Draw a line from the center to the edge of the circle.

3 Move the thumbtack and loop to where these lines meet. Use the pencil and same length of string to mark off a small arc on the edge of the circle.

4 Repeat to mark off another arc, and continue to do this all the way around the circle.

5 Draw two more lines from the center to the outside of the circle, as shown.

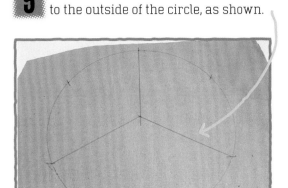

6 Line your ruler up against each of these three lines and draw parallel lines a ruler's width away on either side.

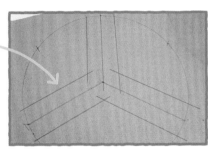

7 Carefully cut out the shape with a utility knife. Cut rounded corners and curve the leading edges over by 0.6 in. (15 mm).

Rounded corners

Bend these edges down

Initial flight path

Boomerang gradually turns in a curved flight path

Rotation

HOW IT WORKS

The long arms of the boomerang give it a **gyroscope** effect, so that it keeps spinning after it is thrown. The curved blades work like a propeller, pushing the boomerang continuously to one side and curving its flight. This is why it eventually returns to the thrower.

Throw the boomerang with a flick of the wrist . . .

. . . be ready for it to come back!

SWISSHH!

AIRY AIRSHIP

Airships are lighter-than-air aircraft. They were the first aircraft capable of controlled, powered flight.

TOOLS:

- Wire cutters
- Needle-nose pliers
- Utility knife
- Craft drill
- White glue
- Ruler
- Pencil
- Scissors
- Double-sided tape

YOU WILL NEED:

Sheet of plain paper

Thin rubber band

Button thread

0.2-in. (5 mm) plastic bead

Helium-filled foil balloon

Wooden skewer, 0.1 in. (3 mm) thick

Two small paper clips

Coffee stirring stick

. . . and you may need modeling clay

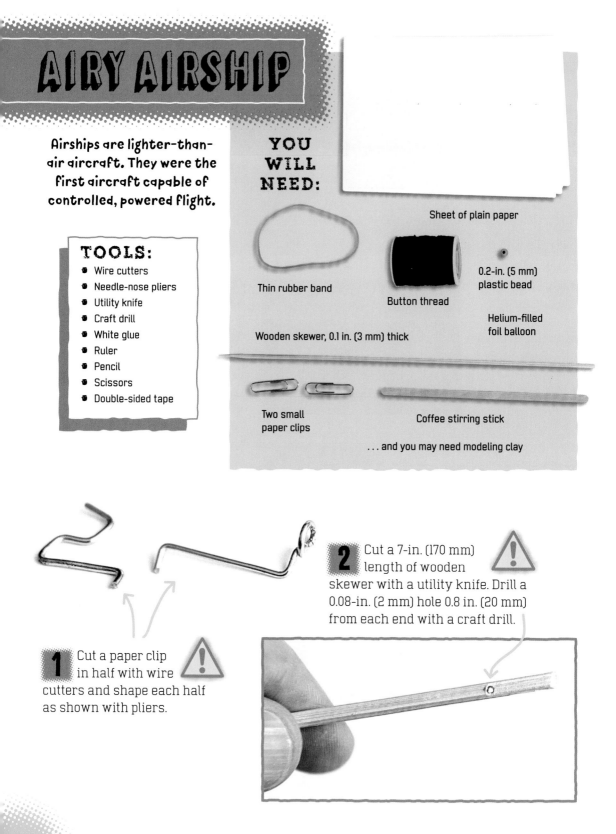

1 Cut a paper clip in half with wire cutters and shape each half as shown with pliers.

2 Cut a 7-in. (170 mm) length of wooden skewer with a utility knife. Drill a 0.08-in. (2 mm) hole 0.8 in. (20 mm) from each end with a craft drill.

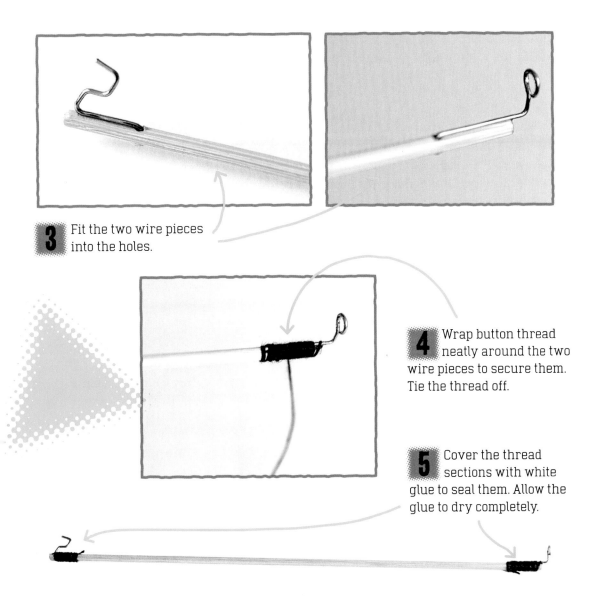

3 Fit the two wire pieces into the holes.

4 Wrap button thread neatly around the two wire pieces to secure them. Tie the thread off.

5 Cover the thread sections with white glue to seal them. Allow the glue to dry completely.

6 Cut a second paper clip in half and make a loop at the end.

Cut a 0.8-in. (20 mm) length from the coffee stirring stick and drill a 0.08-in. (2 mm) hole in the middle.

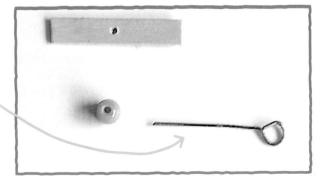

7 Thread the wire through the fixed loop on the skewer, then through the bead, and finally through the hole in the coffee stirrer.

8 Shape the end of the wire as shown and glue it to the stirrer with white glue. This completes the center of the propeller.

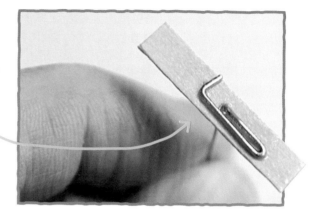

9 Stretch a thin rubber band between the hook on the propeller center and the other end of the skewer.

10 Use the template as a guide to draw and cut out two propeller blades from paper with the measurements given. Glue them to the coffee stirrer.
    Bend over one edge on each by 0.1 in. (3 mm), as shown.

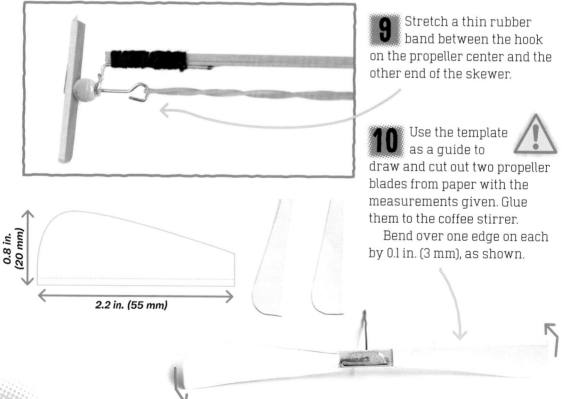

0.8 in. (20 mm)

2.2 in. (55 mm)

11 Attach the balloon to the skewer with double-sided tape. The airship should hang in the air without moving up or down. If not, find the point where the skewer is balanced and add a blob of modeling clay.

Wind up the propeller and release, so your airship will **fly!**

SSSHHH!

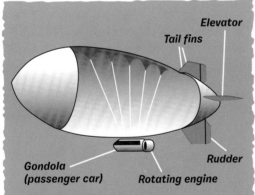

Elevator
Tail fins
Rudder
Gondola (passenger car)
Rotating engine

HOW IT WORKS

The **airship** floats in air just like a submarine floats in water. The balloon is filled with helium, a very low-density gas. The balloon and propeller **displace** exactly the same weight of air as their combined weight, so the airship hangs in the air. The propeller, turned by the rubber band unwinding, pushes air backward, moving the airship forward.

REAL-WORLD ENGINEERING

Early airships were huge envelopes filled with a lifting gas (hydrogen or helium) that was less dense than the air. They were powered by gas engines. Rigid airships were manufactured by the German Zeppelin factory, after whom they were named. From 1928, the enormous airship, LZ-127 *Graf Zeppelin* ran the world's first (and very successful) passenger flight service across the Atlantic Ocean.

FLOATING 'CHUTE

The word "parachute" says it all: para (against), chute (fall). A party tablecloth makes a colorful one!

YOU WILL NEED:

Lightweight plastic tablecloth

String

Heavy washer

TOOLS:
- Long ruler
- Scissors
- Marker

1 Cut a 20-in. (500 mm) square piece of plastic sheet. Fold it in half.

2 Fold in one side from the center to the measurement shown.

10 in. (250 mm)

4.2 in. (106 mm)

3 Repeat on the other side so the edges line up.

4 Cut straight across, so you get a whole, folded triangle.

5 Before you unfold the triangle, mark the six lower corners all around so you can find them easily.

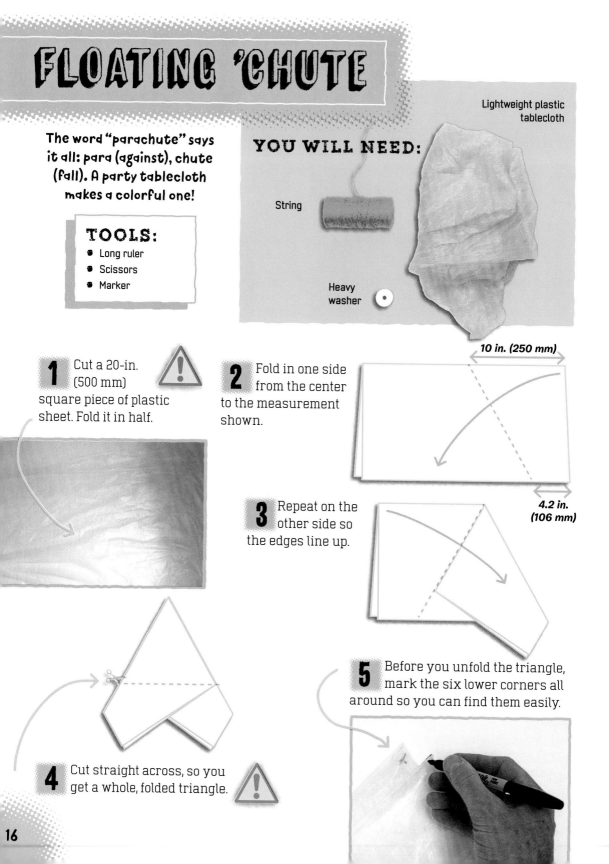

6 Cut 0.8 in. (20 mm) off the top of the triangle (a hole in the center stablizes the parachute's flight). Unfold the triangle to reveal a large hexagon.

7 Cut six lengths of string, 20 in. (500 mm) long. Tie a piece of string to each corner of the 'chute.

8 Gather the strings together so that the corner knots are at even height.

9 Tie a heavy washer to the other ends of the string.

10 Gather the parachute from the center again, then fold it in two a couple of times and wrap the string around it.

Go outside, throw it as high as you can, and watch it drift slowly back to Earth!

HOW IT WORKS

The large surface area of the parachute catches the air as the 'chute falls and provides lots of **drag**. This slows down the payload (whatever it's carrying) to a safe speed. A parachute can be used for dropping goods in remote locations, for saving lives, and even for delivering a spacecraft to a planet's surface! A falling person without a parachute will reach around 120 mph (190 km/h), called the **terminal velocity**. A parachute reduces this speed to a much safer 15–20 mph (25–30 km/h).

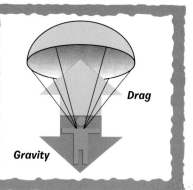

Drag

Gravity

WHIRLING HELICOPTER

Flying a chopper requires special pilot skills. So start by trying out this mini heli. No license required.

TOOLS:
- Ruler
- Kitchen scissors
- White glue
- Small clamps or clothespins
- Craft drill
- Utility knife

YOU WILL NEED:

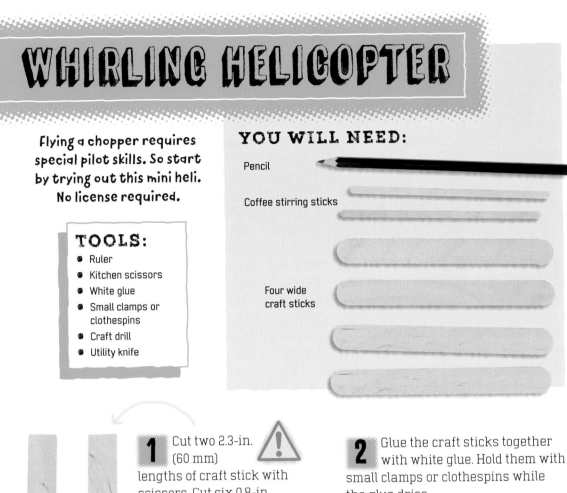

Pencil

Coffee stirring sticks

Four wide craft sticks

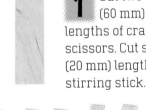

1 Cut two 2.3-in. (60 mm) lengths of craft stick with scissors. Cut six 0.8-in. (20 mm) lengths of coffee stirring stick.

2 Glue the craft sticks together with white glue. Hold them with small clamps or clothespins while the glue dries.

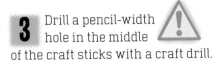

3 Drill a pencil-width hole in the middle of the craft sticks with a craft drill.

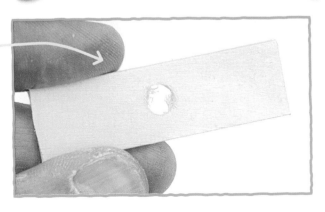

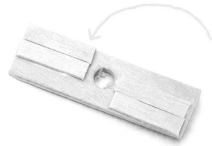

4 Glue four of the coffee stick pieces in place as shown.

5 Glue the remaining two on the outside pieces to make a double layer.

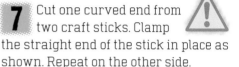

6 Apply a generous layer of white glue, covering the stirrers and stick as shown.

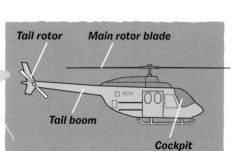

7 Cut one curved end from two craft sticks. Clamp the straight end of the stick in place as shown. Repeat on the other side.

8 Cut the point off of the pencil with a utility knife and discard. Fit the pencil into the hole.

Spin it between the palms of your hands in one direction . . .

FWHIP!

. . . and let it **fly!**

Tail rotor   Main rotor blade

Tail boom

Cockpit

HOW IT WORKS

As the helicopter blades spin, they cut through the air and provide lift. The weight of the pencil holds the blades level so the helicopter flies straight.

HIGH FLYER

Box kites hold the record for the highest flight, at over 16,000 ft. (4,800 m)! They were used in World War II to hold radio aerials in the air and to tow life rafts.

TOOLS:

- Long ruler
- Utility knife
- Hot glue gun
- Skewer or pencil

YOU WILL NEED:

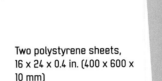

Four 24-in. (600 mm) garden stakes (the thinnest available)

6-in. (150 mm) length of poster tube

Two polystyrene sheets, 16 x 24 x 0.4 in. (400 x 600 x 10 mm)

Nylon garden string

Split ring

2 Use the hot glue gun to glue four pieces together along their narrower edges.

1 Use a utility knife to cut eight equal polystyrene pieces, 12 in. x 8 in. (300 x 200 mm).

3 Repeat to make an exact match for the kite's other half.

4 Use the hot glue gun to glue the garden stakes inside the box corners as shown.

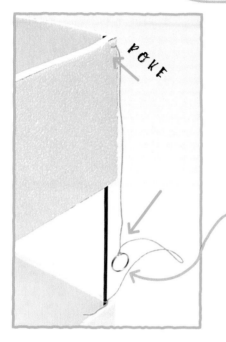

POKE

5 Cut a 28-in. (700 mm) length of string. Make holes in a top corner of the kite with a skewer or pencil point. Push one end of the string in and around the stake and tie it on. Add a split ring to the rest of the string, just above the midpoint, with a crow's foot knot (see page 30). Tie the string to the stake above the lower section.

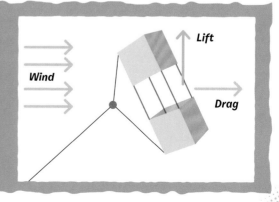

You only need a light wind to get your kite to fly!

6 Tie the end of a 100-ft. (30 m) length of string around the poster tube. Wrap it around the tube, then tie the other end to the split ring with a crow's foot hitch knot (see page 30).

HOW IT WORKS

The box kite design is very stable and works well even in low winds. The forces at work on it are the same as for any other aircraft: lift, weight, and drag. Lift is the force that gets the kite into the air. When wind moves around the box structure, there is more pressure up from the bottom than down from the top, so up it goes. The kite is kept airborne by wind flowing through it.

Lift

Wind

Drag

ORNITHOPTER

This early flying machine was named after the Greek *ornithos*, for "bird," and *pteron*, "wing." They were so-called because people strapped on wings and tried to fly like birds.

TOOLS:

- Craft drill
- Utility knife
- Ruler
- White glue
- Needle-nose pliers
- Compass
- Scissors
- Super glue
- Double-sided tape

YOU WILL NEED:

Heavy rubber band

Corrugated cardboard scrap

Heavy plastic shopping bag

Three 0.2-in. (5 mm) plastic beads

Four 10-in. (250 mm) wooden skewers, 0.1 in. (3 mm) thick

Three craft sticks

Button thread

Small paper clips

Eraser

Coffee stirring sticks

0.08 in. (2 mm) *for the end holes*

0.1 in. (3 mm) *for the inner holes*

0.08 in. (2 mm)

1 Hold together two craft sticks so that they are lined up and drill holes with a craft drill, as shown. Cut the craft sticks down to 3 in. (70 mm) with a utility knife.

2 Cut off two 8-in. (200 mm) lengths of skewer. Thread them onto the craft sticks so the craft sticks are one craft-stick width apart.

3 Cut off a short section of craft stick and glue it into the gap with white glue. This will be the ornithopter body.

4 To make the wings, straighten and then fold two paper clips with pliers to make the dogleg shape shown.

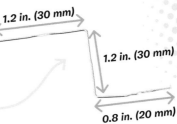

1.2 in. (30 mm)

1.2 in. (30 mm)

0.8 in. (20 mm)

5 Cut two more 8-in. (200 mm) skewers for the wing arms with a utility knife. Cut a notch in one end of each and a groove to fit the center of the wire.

6 Fit a paper clip wire in place on each skewer and wrap button thread around it to secure the wire to the skewer. Tie a knot in the thread and cover it all with white glue to keep it in place. Allow to dry.

7 Fit the wing wires into the small holes on the body. Thread a bead on each and bend the wires around to hold them on.

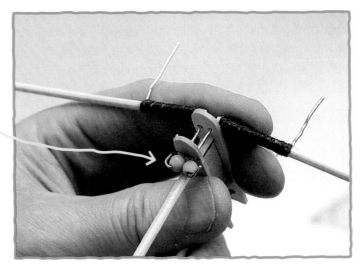

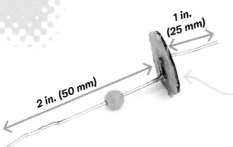

1 in. (25 mm)

2 in. (50 mm)

8 Make another dogleg from a paper clip, as shown. Draw, cut out, and glue on a 0.8-in. (20 mm) circle of cardboard to act as a washer, using super glue. Allow to dry.

9 Fit the wire on the body and make a hook at the end.

10 Straighten out another paper clip, make the hook as shown, and wrap the rest around the back end of the upper skewer.

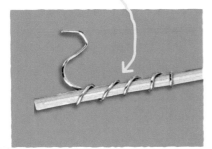

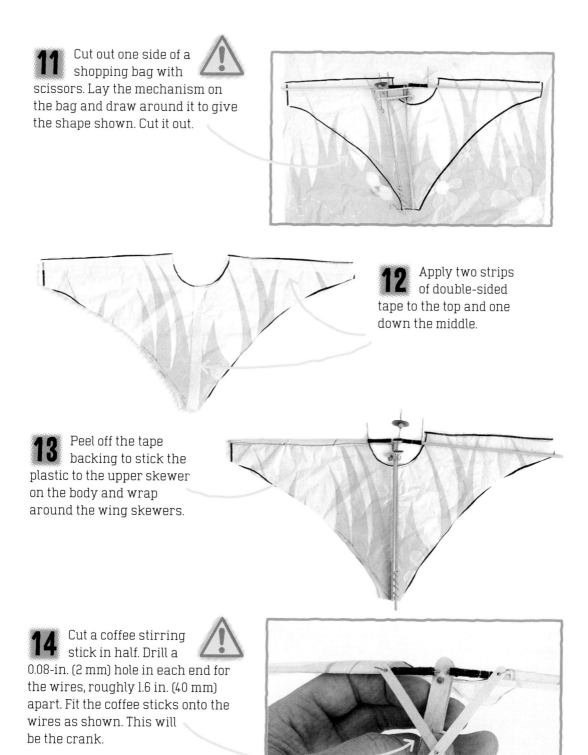

11 Cut out one side of a shopping bag with scissors. Lay the mechanism on the bag and draw around it to give the shape shown. Cut it out.

12 Apply two strips of double-sided tape to the top and one down the middle.

13 Peel off the tape backing to stick the plastic to the upper skewer on the body and wrap around the wing skewers.

14 Cut a coffee stirring stick in half. Drill a 0.08-in. (2 mm) hole in each end for the wires, roughly 1.6 in. (40 mm) apart. Fit the coffee sticks onto the wires as shown. This will be the crank.

15 Bend the wing wires over to secure the coffee sticks. Cut off a small section of eraser and press it over the crank handle to secure it.

Make sure the crank can still move!

16 To make the tail, lay out three whole coffee sticks over plastic, as shown. Draw around them. The plastic shape should be slightly larger all around, except at the top. Cut it out. Use double-sided tape to secure the two edges over the side sticks. Cut a 3-in. (75 mm) piece of coffee stick for the crosspiece. Glue in place with white glue. When dry, trim to fit.

17 Unfold and wrap a paper clip around the end of the central stick, as shown.

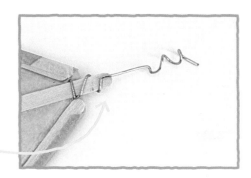

HOW IT WORKS

Ornithopters fly by mimicking the up-and-down flapping of a bird's wings. As the machine travels through the air, the wings push air downward, producing lift. The flapping movement replaces the rotary movement of a propeller or the thrust from a jet engine. Forward movement is provided by the rubber band releasing energy.

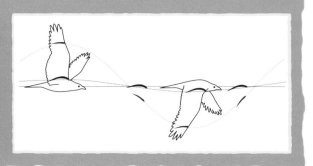

18 Wrap the other end of the tail paper clip around the end of the upper skewer on the body. Attach the rubber band between the two hooks on the lower skewer.

19 Wind up the model by turning the crank handle (wire on the eraser). Throw the ornithopter as you release the crank. Make adjustments to the tail for the best flight.

If it stalls in flight, lower the tail

Normal flight

If it dives in flight, raise the tail

Crank handle

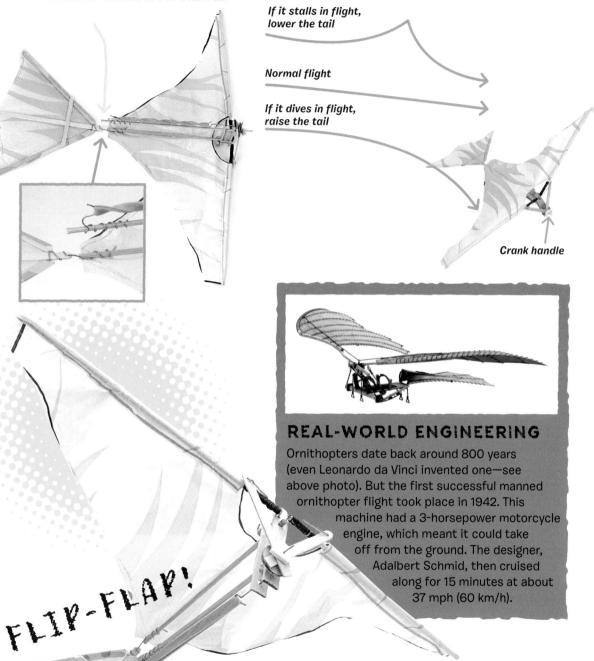

FLIP-FLAP!

REAL-WORLD ENGINEERING

Ornithopters date back around 800 years (even Leonardo da Vinci invented one—see above photo). But the first successful manned ornithopter flight took place in 1942. This machine had a 3-horsepower motorcycle engine, which meant it could take off from the ground. The designer, Adalbert Schmid, then cruised along for 15 minutes at about 37 mph (60 km/h).

AIR-POWERED ROCKET

This rocket is foot—rather than fuel—operated! Standby...3, 2, 1...

TOOLS:
- Craft drill
- Screwdriver
- White glue
- Small clamp
- Utility knife
- Ruler
- Gaffer tape (or duct tape)

YOU WILL NEED:

0.6-in. (15 mm) pipe insulation

0.6-in. (15 mm) pipe

Craft foam

2-liter soda bottle

Craft cork

Two 0.6-in. (15 mm) pipe clips with screws

12-in. (300 mm) length of garden hose

Wood scraps, each about 20 in. (500 mm) long

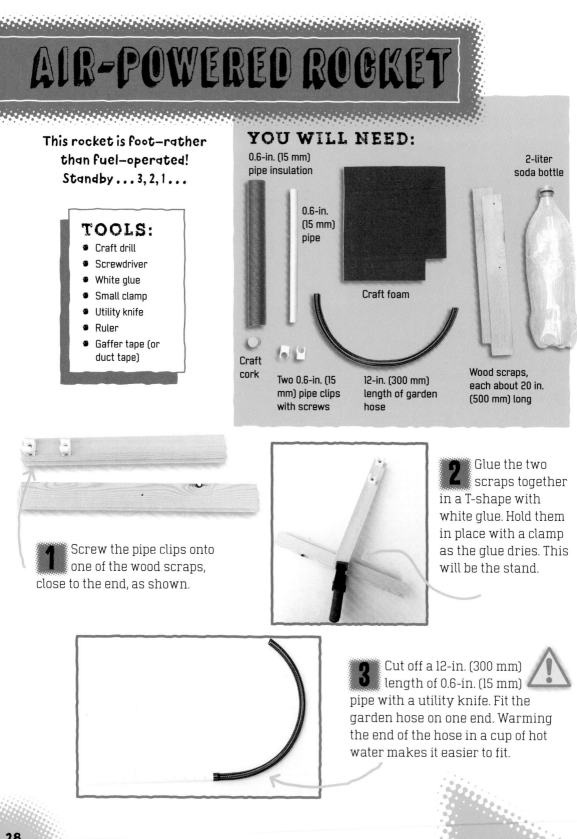

1 Screw the pipe clips onto one of the wood scraps, close to the end, as shown.

2 Glue the two scraps together in a T-shape with white glue. Hold them in place with a clamp as the glue dries. This will be the stand.

3 Cut off a 12-in. (300 mm) length of 0.6-in. (15 mm) pipe with a utility knife. Fit the garden hose on one end. Warming the end of the hose in a cup of hot water makes it easier to fit.

4 Cut a 10-in. (250 mm) length of pipe insulation with a utility knife. Press a cork into the end. This is the rocket body.

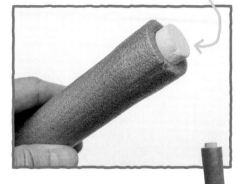

5 Use a utility knife to cut three triangle fin shapes from craft foam, 3.9 x 1.4 x 4.1 in. (100 x 35 x 105 mm). Cut three 4.1-in. (105 mm) slots in the rocket body and fit the fins in place.

6 Clamp the pipe to the stand as shown.
Fit the bottle over the end of the hose and seal it with gaffer tape.

7 Fit the rocket over the pipe.

Stamp on the bottle to launch the rocket into orbit!

FFOOMM!

HOW IT WORKS

Stamping on the bottle forces air into the tube and blows the rocket model straight up. Once airborne, the fins keep it pointing forward as it flies, just as those on a real rocket do. The weight of the cork pulls the front of the rocket around when it reaches the top of its flight and points it back down to Earth

GRAF ZEPPELIN LZ 127 · 7s · POSTES · REPUBLIQUE POPULAIRE REVOLUTIONNAIRE DE GUINÉE · IMPRESSOR S.A. (SWITZERLAND) + P. GAUDARD)

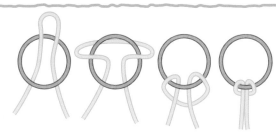

CROW'S FOOT KNOT
(above)

CROW'S FOOT HITCH KNOT
(below)

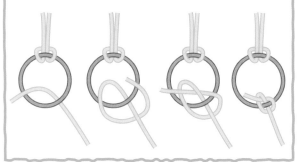

AIR RESISTANCE
(see Drag)

AIRSHIP
An aircraft that is lighter than air, also called an aerostat. It is essentially a bag full of a lighter-than-air gas, but unlike a hot-air balloon, it has its own power. Early airships carried a crew, and the largest airships carried passengers. In time, helium replaced hydrogen—which is flammable—as the lifting gas. This was first done in the United States, where large amounts of helium were first discovered.

There are three main types of airship: non-rigid blimps; semi-rigid, with a supporting structure; and rigid zeppelins. Airships were used less over time as airplane design developed, but they are still made for observation and research, advertising, and tourism, for which their ability to hover for long periods is a big advantage.

DISPLACE
To push aside—as in, the amount of a gas or liquid that is pushed away by an object floating in it

DRAG
A kind of friction that opposes an object's direction of movement and slows it down. Drag is also known as air resistance for objects moving in air, or fluid resistance for objects moving in water.

GYROSOCOPE
A wheel mounted on a spindle within a metal frame. When spinning freely on a flat surface, it stays upright (resisting gravity). It can even maintain a sideways spin and balance on a string. Its ability to resist any change to its spinning direction makes it a vital navigation instrument on airplanes, helicopters, and space probes, as it feeds back information on what a craft's position is, relative to where it should be.

LIFT

The force that opposes the weight of an aircraft to keep it in the air. The flow of air has to be turned by all or some part of the aircraft, and it has to be moving to do this. In airplanes (and birds!), lift is mostly generated by the wings.

LOW DENSITY

A low concentration of mass in a substance. Density is a measure of how much mass there is in a certain volume of a substance. A low-density substance, such as sponge, has a large volume but low mass. Gases have a lower density than liquids or solids. While the density of a liquid or solid remains mostly constant, the density of a gas can vary widely, depending on its temperature and pressure.

ORNITHOPTER

An aircraft that flies by flapping its wings like a bird. These flying machines are usually built to the same scale as a bird. Among the many variations on the design was Lawrence Hargrave's idea for small wings that powered up larger wings. Percival Spencer and Jack Stephenson flew the first successful unmanned ornithopter in 1961. Called the Spencer Orniplane, it had a wingspan of 7 ft. 6.5 in. (2.3 m) and operated with a compact, two-stroke engine.

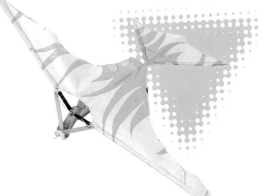

TERMINAL VELOCITY

The fastest speed reached by an object falling through a fluid, such as a skydiver freefalling through air to the ground

THERMAL

An upward current of warm air rising from the ground or a low-lying structure. Warm air near the surface of the ground expands and becomes lighter than the surrounding air, so it rises, gradually cooling until it stops when its temperature is the same as the surrounding air. Urban areas and roads are good sources of thermals. Cumulus clouds often rest at the top of thermals, showing their presence. The clouds may line up in rows, called "cloud streets" by glider pilots.

INDEX

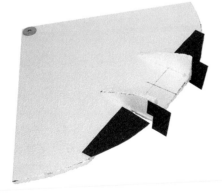

THE AUTHOR

Rob Ives is a former math and science teacher who is currently a designer and paper engineer living in Cumbria, UK. He creates science- and project-based children's books, including *Paper Models that Rock!* and *Paper Automata*. He specializes in character-based paper animations and all kinds of fun and fascinating science projects, and he often visits schools to talk about design technology and to demonstrate his models. Rob's other series for Hungry Tomato include *Tabletop Battles* and *Amazing Science Experiments*.

Picture Credits
(abbreviations: t = top; b = bottom;
c = center; l = left; r = right)
Shutterstock.com: 3Dsculptor
6tr & 29br; Boris15 30tl; Leo
Blanchette 27br; Richard Thornton
9br & 31bl.